The Hanuman Chalisa

THE HANUMAN CHALISA

TULSIDAS

TRANSLATED BY ABHAY K.

BLOOMSBURY
NEW DELHI • LONDON • OXFORD • NEW YORK • SYDNEY

BLOOMSBURY INDIA
Bloomsbury Publishing India Pvt. Ltd
Second Floor, LSC Building No. 4, DDA Complex, Pocket C – 6 & 7,
Vasant Kunj, New Delhi, 110070

BLOOMSBURY, BLOOMSBURY INDIA and the Diana logo
are trademarks of Bloomsbury Publishing Plc

First published in India 2025

Translation copyright © Abhay K., 2025

Abhay K. has asserted his moral right to be identified as the translator
of this work in accordance with the Indian Copyright Act, 1957

The translator's views and interpretations are his own

All rights reserved. No part of this publication may be: i) reproduced
or transmitted in any form, electronic or mechanical, including
photocopying, recording or by means of any information storage
or retrieval system without prior permission in writing from the
publishers; or ii) used or reproduced in any way for the training,
development or operation of artificial intelligence (AI) technologies,
including generative AI technologies. The rights holders expressly
reserve this publication from the text and data mining exception as
per Article 4(3) of the Digital Single Market Directive (EU) 2019/790

ISBN: HB: 978-93-69527-76-2; eBook: 978-93-69527-35-9
2 4 6 8 10 9 7 5 3 1

Typeset in Adobe Caslon Pro by Manipal Technologies Limited
Printed and bound in India by Thomson Press India Ltd

To find out more about our authors and books visit
www.bloomsbury.com and sign up for our newsletters

Introduction

The Hanuman Chalisa is one of the most popular and powerful devotional hymns dedicated to Lord Hanuman. It was composed by Goswami Tulsidas (1511–1623) in the Awadhi language around 1575.

The Bhakti movement was at its peak in North and East India between the fifteenth and seventeenth centuries. It emphasised direct, personal devotion to a chosen deity, with the aim of attaining liberation through love and surrender. Tulsidas primarily followed Saguna Bhakti, focusing on the divine attributes of Lord Rama, inspiring personal devotion. He viewed Hanuman as the epitome of a devotee (bhakta). Hanuman's selfless service, unwavering loyalty, and strength in the face of adversity made him a powerful symbol of bhakti in Tulsidas' eyes. So he accepted Hanuman as his role model and guru, who could lead him to Lord Rama and help him attain spiritual liberation.

The Hanuman Chalisa consists of two opening dohas praising the guru and seeking Hanuman's blessings, forty chaupais and a closing doha for Hanuman's grace and protection. It is recited by millions of devotees for strength, protection and blessings.

TULSIDAS

Goswami Tulsidas was the pen name of Rambola Dubey. As per legend, he was named Rambola because the first words he spoke after his birth were 'Rama, Rama!' Orphaned soon after, he was accepted as a disciple by Narharidas of the Ramananda order and was named Tulsidas.

He became famous after composing the Ramcharitmanas, which he wrote in Awadhi to make the story of Rama more accessible to those who did not know Sanskrit. Legend and folklore have it that Akbar summoned Tulsidas to Fatehpur Sikri to witness his miraculous powers for bringing the dead back to life, which he was believed to possess because of his personal encounters with Lord Rama and Hanuman. However, Tulsidas clarified to Akbar that he did not possess any such powers. Taking it as an insult, the emperor got Tulsidas imprisoned. While in prison, Tulsidas composed the Hanuman Chalisa, hoping that just as Hanuman had helped Sugriva, Vibhishana and Rama, he would help him too, to get out of prison. It is said that soon after he composed the Hanuman Chalisa, a troop of monkeys wreaked havoc in Fatehpur Sikri and continued to do so until Tulsidas was released from prison.

'Chalisa' means forty, referring to the forty verses in the hymn, excluding the introductory and concluding dohas. The composition glorifies Lord Hanuman's strength, devotion, intelligence and divine powers while also seeking his blessings.

LORD HANUMAN

Hanuman was born to Anjana and Kesari. He is known as the son of the deity Vayu, or Pawan (the Wind God), because of legends associated with Vayu's role in Hanuman's birth. Hanuman is said to be an incarnation of Lord Shiva. Also called Maruti (the son of Marut, or the Wind), Bajrangbali (having a body like a thunderbolt) and Anjaneya (Anjana's son), he is celebrated for his unwavering devotion to Lord Rama.

The Anjanadri Hill in Tirumala is considered the birthplace of Hanuman. Anjaneri in Nashik, Maharashtra, and Anjeneri and Anjanadri (near Hampi) in Gangavathi Taluk, Koppal District, Karnataka, are places that claim to be the location of Kishkindha, where Hanuman spent his childhood.

In Vaishnava traditions, Hanuman is not related to Shiva, but he is known as Shiva's avatar in Shaiva traditions. The Shiva Purana mentions Hanuman as an avatar of Shiva; all other puranas and scriptures clearly refer to him as the spiritual son of Vayu or an incarnation of Vayu. The Skanda Purana, a South Indian version of the Shiva Purana, presents Hanuman as the union of Shiva and Vishnu, or as Ayyappa, the son of Shiva and Mohini (the female avatar of Vishnu). The seventeenth-century Odia work 'Rasavinoda' by Dinakrishnadasa mentions that the three gods – Brahma, Vishnu and Shiva – came together to take the form of Hanuman.

'Hanuman' means one who has a disfigured jaw. According to a puranic legend, the infant Hanuman mistakes the sun for a fruit and heroically attempts to reach it. To protect the sun from him, Indra, the king of gods, hurls his thunderbolt at Hanuman, wounding him in the jaw.

In the Muktika Upanishad, Hanuman engages in dialogue with Rama about the subject of moksha.

The earliest mention of a divine monkey is in Hymn 10.86 of the Rigveda, dated between 1500 and 1200 BCE. The twenty-three verses of the hymn form a metaphorical and riddle-filled legend. It is an elaborate dialogue between Indra, his wife Indrani as well as Vrisakapi, a spirited ape.

In Valmiki's Ramayana, Hanuman is a key figure who serves as a helper and messenger for Rama. It is, however, in the late medieval era that his profile becomes more prominent as an exemplary spiritual devotee, particularly after the Ramcharitmanas by Tulsidas. By the fifteenth century, the Bhakti movement and devotional Bhakti Yoga had emerged as a major trend in Hindu culture in North India, and the Ramcharitmanas presented Rama as a Vishnu avatar, a supreme being and a personal god worthy of devotion, with Hanuman as the ideal loving devotee with legendary courage, strength and powers.

In the epic, when Rama and his brother Lakshmana arrive in Kishkindha while searching for Sita, who has been kidnapped by Ravana, Hanuman introduces Rama to Sugriva. Rama helps liberate Sugriva from his brother Vali's captivity and makes him the king of Kishkindha. In return Rama's newfound friend, the monkey king Sugriva, agrees to send his army in all four directions in search of Sita. Sugriva sends Hanuman to the south. Hanuman travels all the way to the southernmost tip of the Indian peninsula, where he encounters the ocean with the island of Lanka (believed to be modern-day Sri Lanka) visible on the horizon.

Hanuman flies across the narrow channel to Lanka, where he discovers a city ruled by the king Ravana and his demon followers. After searching the city, he discovers Sita at an Ashoka grove, guarded by fierce demons. When the demons fall asleep, he meets Sita, introduces himself and tells her how he came to find her. She reveals that Ravana kidnapped her and is forcing her to marry him soon. Hanuman offers to rescue her, but Sita refuses, stating that her husband Rama must do it.

After visiting Sita, Hanuman starts destroying the grove, prompting the demon soldiers to capture him. He is taken to Ravana's court. Ravana orders his servants to wrap an oil-soaked cloth around Hanuman's tail. However, every time they attempt to do so, he grows his tail longer and longer so that more cloth is needed. This continues until Ravana has had enough and orders his tail to be set on fire. Hanuman jumps from rooftop to rooftop, setting ablaze building after building, until much of the city is burning. Then he rushes back to Kishkindha, where Rama has been waiting all along for news of Sita. Hearing that she is safe and is awaiting him, Rama gathers the support of Sugriva's army and marches to Lanka. Thus begins the legendary Battle of Lanka. Throughout the long battle, Hanuman plays the crucial role of a general in the army. During one intense fight, Lakshmana is wounded and can only be revived using the Sanjivani herb from the Himalayas. Being the only one who could make the journey in time to save Lakshmana, Hanuman is sent to bring the herb.

In the end, Rama kills Ravana and the rest of the demon army, returning home to Ayodhya as king along with Sita.

Some envious courtiers in Ayodhya question Hanuman's loyalty to Rama. Hanuman tears open his chest to show his devotion, revealing an image of Rama and Sita etched on his heart.

In the Mahabharata, Bhima, passing through a forest while looking for flowers for his wife, finds a feeble monkey in his way. He asks him to move, but the monkey refuses. Rather, he suggests that Bhima lift his tail. Bhima readily agrees but is unable to lift the monkey's tail. The monkey then reveals himself, much to Bhima's surprise, as Hanuman, and prophesies that Bhima will soon have to fight a bloody war. He promises that he will be present on his brother Arjuna's chariot flag and will protect his chariot during the Kurukshetra war.

SIGNIFICANCE AND IMPACT OF THE HANUMAN CHALISA

Reading or chanting the Hanuman Chalisa regularly invokes Hanuman's blessings, grants courage, strength, wisdom and devotion, and removes fear and negative energy, protecting one from evil, wicked influences and afflictions. It strengthens one's connection with the divine, helps in overcoming obstacles and achieving goals, and brings success and fulfilment, improving mental and physical health, reducing stress and boosting confidence.

The hymn's impact transcends religious ritual – it is a source of inspiration and motivation for millions. Whether in temples, homes or during personal meditation, the Hanuman Chalisa remains a spiritual cornerstone, especially for those seeking courage, focus and resilience while facing life's challenges.

The Hanuman Chalisa is an invaluable guide for navigating the modern world with strength and clarity. Wherever chanted, its verses continue to uplift, protect and empower. The Chalisa glorifies Hanuman as the ideal bhakta, embodying humility, strength and complete surrender. Hanuman is a spiritual master who connects the jiva (soul) to Rama (Supreme Reality).

Though a Rudra avatar (a form of Shiva), Hanuman is Rama's devotee, unifying the followers of Shaivism and Vaishnavism. Hanuman's presence across all yugas emphasises the eternal power of devotion. As the son of Vayu (the Wind God), he represents life-force energy (prana), critical to yoga and inner vitality. The practice of repeating Hanuman's name is seen as protective and purifying. The Chalisa subtly outlines the path of devotion, discipline, humility and strength, leading to liberation.

Contemporary Relevance

Despite being over four centuries old, the Hanuman Chalisa continues to resonate deeply in the modern world, far beyond its original cultural and historical context. Its verses, rich in metaphor and spiritual symbolism, offer guidance, reassurance and empowerment in today's complex, fast-paced life.

A Source of Inner Strength in Times of Uncertainty

In an age marked by stress, anxiety and psychological challenges, the Hanuman Chalisa provides a sense of mental fortitude. Chanting or even silently reading the hymn can have a calming, meditative effect. The invocation of Hanuman's indomitable courage and unwavering focus serves as an emotional anchor when facing personal or professional challenges.

A Tool for Mindfulness and Focus

The Hanuman Chalisa is a powerful tool for mindfulness. When recited, its structured metre, repetition and sacred sound vibrations help still the mind, much like a mantra or breathwork practice. It draws practitioners into the present moment, enhancing concentration and inner awareness.

A Symbol of Selfless Service and Devotion

In an era where growing narcissism and ambition often overshadow community spirit and compassion, Hanuman stands as a timeless ideal of humility and devotion. His service to Lord Rama, without the expectation of reward, reminds us of the power of serving a higher purpose. It is especially relevant for healthcare and public service professionals.

Reclaiming Confidence in the Face of Doubt

Many turn to the Chalisa in moments of self-doubt or fear. Hanuman, who forgot his own divine powers until reminded, is an ideal role model in a world where self-doubt is common. The Chalisa reminds us that strength lies within, waiting to be awakened through self-belief and spiritual awareness.

Universal Appeal Across Cultures and Borders

While rooted in Hindu tradition, the Hanuman Chalisa is now recited and appreciated across the world by people of various backgrounds. Its themes of courage, faith and resilience are universal. It has been translated into multiple languages, set to music across genres and used in everything from yoga classes to motivational speeches. Barack Obama, the former president of the United States of America, carried an image of a Thai Hanuman in his pocket.

The story of Hanuman travelled along with the Indians wherever they went, particularly to Southeast Asia. Hanuman is known as Anuman in Thailand and Andoman in Malaysia. It is believed that the Andaman Islands in the Indian Ocean got their name from Hanuman. In Chinese literature, Hanuman is known as Sun Wukong, an incredible white monkey with miraculous powers, who travels with the Chinese monk Xuanzang to India, protecting him from demons. Many Japanese villages and Shinto temples have a divine monkey (Sarutahiko), who resembles Hanuman, as a protector.

The Bada Mangal festival, during which Hanuman is worshipped every Tuesday from May to June, was started by the nawabs of Lucknow.

TEACHINGS AND ANECDOTES FROM SAINTS ON HANUMAN'S SIGNIFICANCE

Over the centuries, saints, sages and spiritual masters have offered profound insights into the character of Lord Hanuman, elevating him as a model of perfect devotion, unshakable faith and divine strength. Their stories and interpretations add a rich layer of understanding to the recitation of the Hanuman Chalisa.

Tulsidas and the Vision of Hanuman

Tulsidas is said to have had a personal relationship with Lord Hanuman. According to tradition, when Tulsidas longed for a glimpse of Lord Rama, it was Hanuman who guided him to that divine vision. In one account, Hanuman appeared in disguise and directed Tulsidas to the spot where Rama would later appear. It highlights Hanuman's role as a bridge between the devotee and the Divine. Tulsidas says:

'Hanuman is ever present where Rama is worshipped with love.'

Ramana Maharshi on Hanuman's Selflessness

Sri Ramana Maharshi, the sage of Arunachala, often pointed to Hanuman as the epitome of surrender. When asked about the nature of true bhakti (devotion), he cited Hanuman's response to Rama in the Ramayana.

When Rama asked Hanuman, 'How do you see me?' he said:

'As a body, I am your servant; as a soul, I am part of you; but as the Self, I am You.'

This line, deeply mystical in nature, expresses the non-dual understanding that lies at the heart of both bhakti (devotion) and jnana (knowledge).

Neem Karoli Baba and the Living Power of Hanuman

Neem Karoli Baba, a twentieth-century mystic who inspired many (including Ram Dass and Steve Jobs), was a devoted worshipper of Hanuman. He often taught that Hanuman is not a myth but a living force that responds to sincere devotion. He would say:

'Hanuman is the breath of God. When you remember him, he is there.'

Baba emphasised the power of chanting the Hanuman Chalisa regularly, particularly in times of fear, illness or uncertainty. His own life was filled with stories of miraculous healings and protections attributed to Hanuman's grace.

Swami Vivekananda on Hanuman's Strength and Character

Swami Vivekananda admired Hanuman for his character, strength and fearlessness. He regarded Hanuman as representing the ideal of brahmacharya (practising celibacy and self-discipline) and service without ego. He once said:

'If you want strength, look to Hanuman. His very name is a mantra for fearlessness and service.'

Vivekananda urged the youth to follow Hanuman's example not in physical power alone but in mental and spiritual strength.

A Lesson from the Ramayana: Hanuman's Humility

In one lesser-known tale, after the battle in Lanka, Rama began praising Hanuman publicly for all his deeds. Hanuman, overwhelmed, bowed his head and said:

'I am just your servant. I only did what was natural.'

Even after leaping across oceans and defeating demons, Hanuman remains utterly humble. It teaches us that true power is not boastful – it is silent, steady and rooted in humility.

Across traditions, Hanuman emerges not just as a deity but also as a spiritual guide – a reminder that devotion and service can lead to liberation. For saints and seekers alike, Hanuman is the embodiment of the divine potential in each one of us, awakened through love and surrender.

I was introduced to the Hanuman Chalisa during my school days and have been reciting it since then. I have sought solace in it during times of distress and it has benefited me immensely. Lately, I came across a number of English translations of the Hanuman Chalisa, which inspired me to produce my own poetic translation while retaining the energy, flow and rhythm of the original Awadhi text by Tulsidas. I hope my rendering of the Hanuman Chalisa helps readers across the globe access its immense power and positivity.

The Hanuman Chalisa

|| Doha ||

श्रीगुरु चरन सरोज रज, निज मन मुकुर सुधारि।
बरनउँ रघुबर बिमल जसु, जो दायकु फल चारि॥

shri guru charan saroj raj, nij man mukur sudhari
barnaun raghubar bimal jasu, jo dayaku phal chari

- श्रीगुरु चरन सरोज रज/shri guru charan saroj raj: the dust of the lotus feet of the guru; lotus feet symbolise spiritual purity and enlightenment
- फल चारि/phal chari: the four fruits are dharma (righteousness), artha (wealth), kama (desire) and moksha (liberation)

1

With the dust from the lotus feet of Guru,
I cleanse my mind's core
Describing Rama's glory pure
who gives us fruits four

बुद्धिहीन तनु जानिके, सुमिरौं पवन-कुमार।
बल बुद्धि विद्या देहु मोहिं, हरहु कलेस बिकार॥

buddhihin tanu janike, sumirau pavan-kumar
bal buddhi vidya dehu mohin, harahu kales bikaar

- बुद्धि/buddhi: intellect; हीन/hin: lacking; तनु/tanu: body or form; जानिके/janike: knowing
- सुमिरौं/sumirau: I remember or meditate upon; पवन-कुमार/pavan-kumar: son of the Wind God
- बल/bal: strength; विद्या/vidya: knowledge; देहु/dehu: grant; मोहिं/mohin: to me
- हरहु/harahu: remove; कलेस/kales: troubles, afflictions; बिकार/bikaar: impurities, distortions

2

Son of Wind, being ignorant I pray
Grant me strength, intellect and wisdom,
Take my troubles and flaws away

|| Chalisa ||

जय हनुमान ज्ञान गुन सागर।
जय कपीस तिहुँ लोक उजागर॥

jai hanuman gyan gun sagar
jai kapis tihun lok ujagar

- ज्ञान गुन सागर/gyan gun sagar: ocean of knowledge and virtue
- कपीस/kapis: lord of the monkeys; metaphorically, master of the senses
- तिहुँ लोक/tihun lok: the three realms, heaven, earth and netherworld

1

Jai Hanuman, the ocean of knowledge
Jai Kapis, all the three realms ablaze

राम दूत अतुलित बल धामा।
अंजनि पुत्र पवनसुत नामा॥

rama-doot atulit bal dhama
anjani putra pavan-sut nama

- राम दूत /rama-doot: messenger of Lord Rama
- अतुलित बल धामा/atulit bal dhama: abode of immeasurable strength
- अंजनी पुत्र/anjani putra: son of Anjani
- पवनसुत/pavan-sut: son of the Wind God, indicating agility and spiritual breath

2

Rama's man of unparalleled might
Son of Anjani, the Wind's delight

महावीर विक्रम बजरंगी।
कुमति निवार सुमति के संगी॥

mahavir vikram bajrangi
kumati nivar sumati ke sangi

- बजरंगी/bajrangi: one with the strength of a thunderbolt
- कुमति/सुमति/kumati/sumati: folly/wisdom

3

Mighty warrior, brave and burly
Wisdom's ally, dispeller of folly

कंचन बरन बिराज सुबेसा।
कानन कुंडल कुंचित केसा॥

kanchan baran biraj subesa
kanan kundal kunchit kesa

- कंचन बरन/kanchan baran: golden complexion
- सुबेसा/subesa: auspicious attire
- कानन कुंडल/kanan kundal: wearing earrings
- कुंचित केसा/kunchit kesa: curly hair, signifying vitality and strength

4

Glowing as gold, in pleasing attire
Wearing earrings, curly hair

हाथ बज्र औ ध्वजा बिराजै।
काँधे मूँज जनेउ साजै॥

hath bajra aur dhvaja birajai
kandhe moonj janeu sajai

- बज्र/bajra: thunderbolt (symbol of strength); associated with Indra
- ध्वजा/dhvaja: flag, often symbolic of victory and righteousness
- मूँज जनेऊ/moonj janeu: a sacred thread made of munja grass, showing his adherence to Vedic discipline

5

Thunderbolt, victory flag holder
Sacred thread adorning your shoulder

शंकर सुवन केसरी नंदन।
तेज प्रताप महा जग वंदन॥

shankar suvan kesari nandan
tej pratap maha jag vandan

- शंकर सुवन/shankar suvan: offspring of Shiva; Hanuman is often regarded as a form or emanation of Shiva
- तेज प्रताप/tej pratap: majestic brilliance and power
- जग वंदन/jag vandan: revered by the world; shows Hanuman's universal significance

6

Shiva's incarnation, Kesari's wonder
The world bows to your splendour

विद्यावान गुनी अति चातुर।
राम काज करिबे को आतुर॥

vidyavan guni ati chatur
rama kaj karibe ko aatur

- विद्यावान/vidyavan: endowed with knowledge; symbolises the union of wisdom and devotion
- गुनी/guni: possessor of good qualities; an ethical being
- चातुर/chatur: clever or skilful, showing that spiritual strength also requires mental acuity
- राम काज करिबे को आतुर/rama kaj karibe ko aatur: eager to serve Rama; this phrase defines Hanuman's selfless action and devotion

7

Erudite, virtuous and immensely clever
Eager to fulfil Rama's commands ever

प्रभु चरित्र सुनिबे को रसिया।
राम लखन सीता मन बसिया॥

prabhu charitra sunibe ko rasiya
rama lakhan sita man basiya

- प्रभु चरित्र/prabhu charitra: Lord Rama's character in the Ramayana; Hanuman delights in divine narratives, symbolising devotion through listening
- मन बसिया/man basiya: residing in the mind; Rama, Lakshmana and Sita live in Hanuman's heart, representing a state of inner union

8

Earnest to hear the Lord's tale
Rama, Lakshmana, Sita in your heart dwell

सूक्ष्म रूप धरि सियहि दिखावा।
बिकट रूप धरि लंक जरावा॥

sookshm roop dhari siyahi dikhava
bikat roop dhari lank jarava

- सूक्ष्म रूप/sookshm roop: a subtle or minuscule form taken to reach Sita; represents humility and adaptability in service
- बिकट रूप/bikat roop: a terrifying form used to burn Lanka; a symbol of righteous wrath used to uphold dharma – reflects the dual aspects of divinity (compassion and fierce energy)

9

Appearing to Sita in your subtle avatar
Taking majestic form you set Lanka on fire

भीम रूप धरि असुर संहारे।
रामचंद्र के काज संवारे॥

bhima roop dhari asur sanhare
ramachandra ke kaj sanvare

- भीम रूप/bhima roop: gigantic and fearsome form; Bhima evokes destructive strength
- असुर संहारे/asur sanhare: destruction of demons; a metaphor for destroying inner demons – ego, ignorance, lust
- काज संवारे/kaj sanvare: fulfilling Rama's mission, representing a devotee's alignment with divine will

10

Assuming fierce form you slayed fiends
Accomplishing Rama's noble ends

लाय सजीवन लखन जियाये।
श्री रघुबीर हरषि उर लाये॥

laye sajivan lakhan jiyaye
shri raghubeer harashi ur laye

- सजीवन/sajivan: the Sanjivani herb, a metaphor for life-giving force; it means Hanuman revives lost faith or hope
- हरषि उर लाए/harashi ur laye: Rama embraces Hanuman in joy, showing the highest reward of bhakti is divine grace

11

Bringing Sanjivani, you revived Lakshmana
Joyous Rama embraced you with affection

रघुपति कीन्ही बहुत बड़ाई।
तुम मम प्रिय भरतहि सम भाई॥

raghupati keenhi bahut badhai
tum mam priya bharat-hi sam bhai

- प्रिय भरतहि सम भाई/priya bharat-hi sam bhai: as beloved to me as my brother Bharat

12

Rama heaped you with profuse praise, rather
'You're beloved to me as Bharat, my brother'

सहस बदन तुम्हरो जस गावैं।
अस कहि श्रीपति कंठ लगावैं॥

sahas badan tumharo jas gaave
as kahi shripati kanth lagaave

- सहस बदन /sahas badan: the thousand-headed singing your glory; it indicates divine praise, a metaphor for the cosmic serpent Shesha, a mount of Vishnu
- अस कहि श्रीपति कंठ लगावैं/as kahi shripati kanth lagaave: embraced by Rama, who is an avatar of Shri-pati (Vishnu) himself

13

'The thousand-headed sings your praise'
Saying so Rama holds you in his
embrace

सनकादिक ब्रह्मादि मुनीसा।
नारद सारद सहित अहीसा॥

sankadik brahmadi munisa
narad sarad sahit aheesa

- सनकादिक/sankadik: the four mind-born sons of Brahma; eternal sages
- ब्रह्मादि मुनीसा/brahmadi munisa: Brahma and other sages
- नारद सारद सहित अहीसा/narad sarad sahit aheesa: including Narad, Saraswati and the cosmic serpent Shesha

14

Sanak, Brahma and other sages
Narada, Saraswati, Shesha since ages

जम कुबेर दिगपाल जहाँ ते।
कवि कोविद कहि सके कहाँ ते॥

jam kuber digpal jahan te
kavi kovid kahi sake kahan te

- दिगपाल/digpal: guardians of the directions
- कवि/kavi: poet
- कोविद/kovid: scholar

15

Yama, Kubera, Digpala, all full of your praise
That poets and scholars, none can upraise

तुम उपकार सुग्रीवहि कीन्हा।
राम मिलाय राज पद दीन्हा॥

tum upkar sugrivahi kinha
rama milaye rajpad dinha

- उपकार/upkar: a benevolent deed; Hanuman plays a key role in restoring dharma
- सुग्रीवहि कीन्हा/Sugrivahi kinha: helped Sugriva regain his kingdom, symbolising Hanuman as a diplomat
- राम मिलाय/Rama milaye: uniting Sugriva with Rama suggests the devotee's role in uniting estranged souls with the Divine
- राज पद दीन्हा/rajpad dinha: granting kingship is symbolic of spiritual sovereignty or moksha

16

Amity between Rama and Sugriva sown
You helped him to reclaim his throne

तुम्हरो मंत्र विभीषण माना।
लंकेश्वर भए सब जग जाना॥

tumharo mantra vibhishana maana
lankeshwar bhaye sab jag jaana

- मंत्र/mantra: advice or spiritual counsel; Hanuman's counsel leads to right action
- विभीषण माना/Vibhishana mana: Vibhishana, by accepting Hanuman's words, chooses dharma over blood ties
- लंकेश्वर/Lankeshwar: Lord of Lanka; metaphorically showing that surrendering to truth leads to divine reward
- सब जग जाना/sab jag jaana: Hanuman's influence and righteousness are universally acknowledged

17

Vibhishana receiving your counsel sane
The world knows, gained Lanka's reign

जुग सहस्त्र योजन पर भानू।
लील्यो ताहि मधुर फल जानू॥

yug sahastra yojan par bhanu
lilyo taahi madhur phal janu

- जुग सहस्त्र योजन/jug sahastra yojan: a hyperbolic distance, symbolising great aspiration; thousands of yojanas
- भानू/bhanu: the sun
- लील्यो/lilyo: swallowed it; as a child, Hanuman mistook the sun for a fruit

18

Million miles away, the sun shone brightly
Taking it as a sweet fruit, you gulped it lightly

प्रभु मुद्रिका मेलि मुख माहीं।
जलधि लाँघि गये अचरज नाहीं॥

prabhu mudrika meli mukh maahi
jaladhi langhi gaye acharaj naahi

- मुद्रिका/mudrika: Rama's ring
- जलधि लाँघि/jaladhi langhi: crossing the ocean of worldly existence
- अचरज नाहीं/acharaj naahi: no wonder

19

Keeping the Lord's ring in your mouth
No wonder, you leapt over the ocean south

दुर्गम काज जगत के जेते।
सुगम अनुग्रह तुम्हरे तेते॥

durgam kaj jagat ke jete
sugam anugrah tumhare tete

- दुर्गम/durgam: difficult or insurmountable tasks in the world
- सुगम/sugam: made easy by Hanuman's grace
- अनुग्रह/anugrah: divine favour

20

All the world's tasks contorted
With your grace get easily sorted

राम दुआरे तुम रखवारे।
होत न आज्ञा बिनु पैसारे॥

rama duaare tum rakhvare
hot na aagya binu paisare

- राम दुआरे/Rama duaare: gatekeeper to Rama
- आज्ञा बिनु/aagya binu: without his permission, no one enters divine grace

21

You stand guard at Rama's abode
No one can enter without your nod

सब सुख लहै तुम्हारी सरना।
तुम रक्षक काहू को डर ना॥

sab sukh lahai tumhari sarna
tum rakshak kahu ko darna

- सरना/sarna: refuge or surrender, a key tenet of bhakti yoga
- तुम रक्षक/tum rakshak: when Hanuman protects, fear dissolves

22

Boundless bliss flows in your haven
Why fear when you're the guardian

आपन तेज सम्हारो आपै।
तीनों लोक हाँक तें काँपै॥

aapan tej samharo aapai
teenon lok haank te kaanpai

- तेज/tej: divine radiance or spiritual power
- तीनों लोक/teenon lok: all three realms
- काँपै/kaanpai: tremble

23

Only you can rein in your splendour
Three worlds tremble when you thunder

भूत पिशाच निकट नहीं आवै।
महाबीर जब नाम सुनावै॥

bhoot pishach nikat nahi aave
mahabeer jab naam sunave

- भूत पिशाच/bhoot pishach: ghosts and evil spirits; symbolic of internal negativities (fear, doubt, temptation)
- नाम सुनावै/naam sunave: chanting Hanuman's name acts as a spiritual shield

24

Hearing your name – the warrior of might
Ghost, spirits take hasty flight

नासै रोग हरै सब पीरा।
जपत निरंतर हनुमत बीरा॥

naase rog hare sab peera
japat nirantar hanumat beera

- नासै रोग/naase rog: diseases disappear, a metaphor for both physical illness and spiritual suffering
- जपत निरंतर/japat nirantar: constantly remembering that Hanuman cures sorrow

25

Chanting Brave Hanuman – again and again
Destroys diseases and takes away pain

संकट तें हनुमान छुड़ावै।
मन क्रम बचन ध्यान जो लावै॥

sankat te hanuman chhudave
man kram bachan dhyan jo lave

- संकट/sankat: crisis or trouble
- मन क्रम बचन/man kram bachan: through mind, action and speech; total devotion
- ध्यान/dhyan: meditation on Hanuman leads to inner liberation

26

Invoking Hanuman in mind, words and action
Brings everyone quick liberation

सब पर राम तपस्वी राजा।
तिन के काज सकल तुम साजा॥

sab par rama tapasvi raja
tin ke kaj sakal tum saja

- राम तपस्वी राजा/Rama tapasvi raja: Rama as a king and ascetic merges kingship with austerity
- सकल तुम साजा/sakal tum saja: Hanuman completes all divine work, symbolising the active arm of God in the world

27

The ascetic king Rama reigns above all
You accomplish all his tasks tall

और मनोरथ जो कोई लावै।
सोई अमित जीवन फल पावै॥

aur manorath jo koi lave
soee amit jeevan phal pave

- मनोरथ/manorath: desires (especially spiritual or dharmic ones)
- अमित जीवन फल/amit jeevan phal: infinite life fruits or liberation

28

Whoever makes wishes sincere
Gains immortal life's elixir

चारों जुग परताप तुम्हारा ।
है परसिद्ध जगत उजियारा ॥

charo jug partap tumhara
hai parasiddha jagat ujiyara

- चारों जुग/charo jug: all four ages (Satya, Treta, Dvapara, Kali); Hanuman is present in each one of these
- जगत उजियारा/jagat ujiyara: his light illuminates the world; symbolic of wisdom spreading through bhakti

29

All the four ages with your glory resound
All the realms with your light abound

साधु सन्त के तुम रखवारे ।
असुर निकन्दन राम दुलारे ॥

sadhu sant ke tum rakhware
asur nikandan rama dulare

- साधु सन्त/sadhu sant: saints and seekers; Hanuman protects them all
- असुर निकन्दन/asur nikandan: destroyer of demons; remover of inner and outer evil
- राम दुलारे/Rama dulare: Rama's beloved

30

The protector of saints and sages
Demon slayer, Rama's beloved since ages

अष्टसिद्धि नौ निधि के दाता।
अस बर दीन जानकी माता॥

ashta siddhi nau nidhi ke data
as bar deen janaki mata

- अष्ट सिद्धि/ashta siddhi: the eight yogic perfections (as per Patanjali and Tantric texts) are Anima (becoming minute), Mahima (becoming vast), Garima (becoming heavy), Laghima (becoming light), Prapti (attaining what is desired), Prakamya (fulfilling desires), Ishitva (lordship) and Vashitva (control over others)
- नौ निधि/nau nidhi: the nine treasures in Vedic cosmology (Padma, Mahapadma, Sankha, Makara, Kacchapa, Mukunda, Kunda, Nila and Kharva); these are symbolic of spiritual abundance
- जानकी माता/Janaki Mata: Sita, consort of Rama, grants Hanuman this boon; divine feminine energy (Shakti) empowering the masculine (Hanuman) energy

31

The bestower of eight perfections
and nine treasures
Mother Sita granted you the boons
beyond measure

राम रसायन तुम्हरे पासा ।
सदा रहो रघुपति के दासा ॥

rama rasayan tumhare pasa
sada raho raghupati ke dasa

- राम रसायन/Rama rasayan: Rama's elixir; a metaphor for immortality through devotion, a bhakti-alchemy that transforms the soul
- रघुपति के दासा/Raghupati ke dasa: eternal servant of Rama; a sacred attitude of selfless service

32

You have Rama's sweet concoction
Ever remain in his true devotion

तुम्हरे भजन राम को पावै ।
जनम जनम के दुख बिसरावै ॥

tumhare bhajan rama ko paave
janam janam ke dukh bisrave

- भजन /bhajan: devotional singing
- राम को पावै/Rama ko paave: through Hanuman's worship, one attains Rama
- जनम जनम के दुख/janam janam ke dukh: the sorrows of countless births are forgotten

33

Singing your name, Rama is found
Easing many births' grief profound

अन्त काल रघुबर पुर जाई।
जहाँ जन्म हरिभक्त कहाई॥

anta-kaal raghubar pur jaee
jaha janma hari-bhakta kahaee

- अन्त काल/anta-kaal: at the time of death
- रघुबर पुर/Raghubar pur: Rama's earthly abode Ayodhya or his spiritual abode Vaikuntha
- हरिभक्त/Hari-bhakta: the Lord's devotee

34

Death will take us to Rama's abode
Where we'll be born as devotees of God

और देवता चित्त न धरई।
हनुमत सेइ सर्व सुख करई॥

aur devata chitt na dharai
hanumat sei sarv sukh karai

- चित्त न धरई/chitt na dharai: no need to meditate on other deities; this isn't exclusivism but emphasis on focused devotion
- सर्व सुख करई/sarv sukh karai: Hanuman grants all joys, material and spiritual

35

Don't meditate upon other deities
Hanuman alone brings all the gaieties

संकट कटै मिटै सब पीरा।
जो सुमिरै हनुमत बलबीरा॥

sankat kate mite sab peera
jo sumire hanumat balbeera

- संकट कटै/sankat kate: troubles are removed
- सुमिरै/sumire: remembering or invoking
- बलबीरा/balbeera: mighty hero

36

Performing mighty Hanuman's incantation
Removes all the troubles and affliction

जय जय जय हनुमान गोसाईं।
कृपा करहु गुरुदेव की नाईं॥

jai jai jai hanuman gosai
kripa karahu gurudev ki nai

- गोसाईं/gosai: a revered master
- गुरुदेव की नाईं/Gurudev ki nai: a divine teacher; Hanuman is considered a guru, being the dispeller of darkness ('gu' meaning darkness; 'ru' meaning remover)

37

Victory to Hanuman, the sovereign
Great Guru, let your blessings rain

जो सत बार पाठ कर कोई।
छूटहि बंदि महा सुख होई॥

jo sat baar paath kar koi
chhutehi bandi maha sukh hoi

- सत बार/sat baar: reciting a hundred times
- छूटहि बंदि/chhutehi bandi: one is freed from bondage – of karma, desires and the cycle of birth
- महा सुख/maha sukh: the bliss of liberation or divine union

38

Whoever recites it a hundred times
Will be liberated and hear blissful chimes

जो यह पढ़ै हनुमान चालीसा।
होय सिद्धि साखी गौरीसा॥

jo yah padhe hanuman chalisa
hoye siddhi sakhi gaurisa

- सिद्धि/siddhi: spiritual attainment or completion of goals
- साखी गौरीसा/sakhi gaurisa: Shiva (Lord of Gauri/Parvati) is witness; implying divine endorsement; Hanuman is a manifestation of Shiva, thus bringing together Shaiva and Vaishnava devotion

39

Hanuman's forty verses, whoever reads these
Will spiritually awaken, Shiva agrees

तुलसीदास सदा हरि चेरा।
कीजै नाथ हृदय महँ डेरा॥

tulsidas sada hari chera
keejai naath hriday mah dera

- हरि चेरा/Hari chera: Tulsidas declares himself a servant of Hari (Vishnu/Rama)
- हृदय महँ डेरा/hriday mah dera: prays that the Lord may dwell in his heart – a classic bhakti motif of the inner temple

40

Tulsidas, forever a devotee of God
Prays, 'Always dwell in my heart, O Lord'

|| Doha ||

पवन तनय संकट हरन मंगल मूरती रूप।
राम लखन सीता सहित हृदय बसहु सुर भूप॥

pavan tanaya sankat haran mangal moorti roop
rama lakhan sita sahit hriday basahu sur bhoop

- पवन तनय/pavan tanaya: son of the Wind God, symbol of prana (life force)
- संकट हरन/sankat haran: remover of obstacles (a role similar to Ganesha's)
- मंगल मूरति/mangal moorti: embodiment of auspiciousness
- राम लखन सीता सहित/Rama Lakhan Sita sahit: with the whole divine family; unity of dharma (Rama), strength (Lakshmana) and grace (Sita)
- हृदय बसहु/hriday basahu: dwell in my heart

Son of Wind, remover of obstacles,
bliss personified
Along with Rama, Lakshmana and Sita,
O King of Gods, in my heart reside.

Acknowledgements

I am grateful to Dhanya Madhavan Nair for going through the manuscript carefully and offering her valuable suggestions.